1 ... ...ince

I Got Older

Written by students
at Curtis Bishop Middle School

Foreword by K. Curtis Lyle

Published by StudioSTL

This book is a publication of StudioSTL, a literary arts center for students and community. StudioSTL empowers youth, ages 6 to 18, by helping them discover, develop, and celebrate their individual voices through writing. We believe a toolbox of writing skills – whether for fun, for school, in personal or professional life – is an indispensable lifelong gift. We bring writers, artists and educators together with students to work on writing and publishing projects that build writing skills and heighten awareness of writing as a magical art. Best of all, because we rely on the dedicated efforts of trained volunteers, we are able to offer free student programming, which we hope keeps our young writers coming back for more.

StudioSTL gratefully acknowledges the Missouri Arts Council for their support of this publication and StudioSTL writing programs.

Published June 2008 by StudioSTL.
ISBN 0-9795112-1-6

All student authors attended seventh-grade at Bishop Middle School, Wellston, Missouri during the writing and publication of this book.

Project Directors: Tess Thompson and Jason Vasser
Classroom Teacher: Matt Picard
Writing Mentors: Betty Burnett, Rae Draizen, Emma Jehle, Jeanne Sabbert Smith, Braden Welborn
Editor: Julie Dill

Photography copyright © 2008 by Elie Gardner.
Book design & Production: Mason Miller.
Printed in the United States of America by Edwards Brothers, Inc., Ann Arbor, Michigan.

Financial assistance for this project has been provided by the Missouri Arts Council, a state agency.

CONTRIBUTORS

Perry Green
Dasia Rice
LaQuonn Williams
Najae Jordan
I'Esha Davis
DaeJohn Wilson
Alexus Shockley
Kamika Nelson
Darrien Daniels
Kenyatta Smith
Deven Simms
Jamie Davis
Kathon Robinson
Brandi George
Jevon Cannon
Darrion Stinson
Thomas Jackson
Michelle Stokes
Cameshia Mays
De'Carla Latchison

Tommie Wilson
Tinisha Hardwrict
Shanika Price
Alexis Cole
Aeriona Watts
Robin Edwards
LeTrell Crews
Adayshia Jackson
Darrion Stinson
Kevin McLemore
Cushsure Hall
Jamonica Gallion
DuShai Jackson
Roderick Reed
Deyon Smith
Tanzania Taylor
James Bush
Antonio Pulliam
Adam Moore
Kaimen Pascall
Tinesha McLemore

K. Curtis Lyle

What's Really Going On!

Stop the world! Take an hour or two out of your busy day and let these young writers conduct you along the high road from body to mind, from soul to spirit, and then back again. They'll pick you up from the place where you relax in the evening; it might be the special thinking spot in the middle of your sofa; it could be the leaning place where you settle every other night in your favorite rocking chair; they'll meet you after dinner under the low soft light of the kitchen table; their poems, songs and stories can even come alive in your bedroom a hour before you pass off into the land of nod. In this original and courageous book readers can create a small magical place for themselves to—in the words of one of the young poets—"block out the madness."

Studio STL Executive Director Elizabeth Ketcher has built a formidable team in classroom teacher Matt Picard, of Teach For America, project directors Tess Thompson and Jason Vasser, and photographer Elie Gardner. They have managed to lay the groundwork for these young people to initiate and organize their inner worlds in ways that are creative, coherent and real. "Real" is a favored word among youth these days, but here we have examples of reality fused to certainty. The equation produces a powerful sound. This is the sound of young men and women speaking truth. The amazing thing about the work is the tone of responsibility that runs through it like an unstoppable river. My grand-mother had a unique way of expressing her sense of someone taking total responsibility for their thoughts and actions. She would say that a person's "love is a rock." She wouldn't say that their love is "like" a rock. She'd say that their love "is" a rock! By that, she meant balanced and just and sure. That feeling is on display everywhere in the writings of these beautiful children.

The words here are both eloquent and plainspoken. They speak of what we would call the normal feelings and pursuits of youth; there are playful memories of sports competition and trips to the mall; some think deeply about family relationships – some stable, some destroyed – and the constant pressure of being pushed and pulled by the glamorous seductions of the material world and by the pressure of peers. When a seventh grader begins a poem with the line, "I wonder who I am inside," continues with, "people tell me I'm intelligent, respectful and loyal," and then ends, "But I tell myself that I'm nothing but a seventh grader inside," we've encountered something akin to a lament. There is a certain elemental sadness here. It's as if one had just encountered an old soul.

Another powerful theme that runs through the book is completion, the need – or the sheer will, one might say – to make the self whole. This is not an unusual quest in human beings, but in people so young I find it both admirable and a little disturbing. Why should they have to use their will in this way? Why should they have to rush past their wants in order to fulfill their needs?

There is a sea change taking place in this country, in this city, in a neighborhood in North St. Louis. Here, at Bishop Middle School, children reflect profoundly, are self-critical, set high expectations for themselves and others, and adhere to the letter and energy of a code which can be defined as faith in themselves.

Read this book if you want to know what's really going on.

K. Curtis Lyle
May 2008

No rubric can quantify the courage necessary to sit down and commit oneself to sincere expression or the joy borne out succeeding in its pursuit. Many of the students asked of themselves during this process, "Who am I?" In response, I'd say you are writers. And I am proud of you.

Matt Picard
7th Grade English Teacher
Bishop Middle School

Perry Green

I Wonder

I wonder who I am
inside.

People tell me I'm
something bigger.

I will never know until
it happens.

People tell me I'm intelligent,
respectful, and loyal.

But I tell myself that I'm
nothing but a 7th grader.

Dasia Rice

There's a Person Who I Love

There's a person who is tall, light-skinned, and who has short hair. There's a person who lives in Wellston and likes it out here. A person who has two kids and who is a single parent. A person who puts clothes and shoes on her kids' bodies to make sure that we are taken care of every day. A person who buys food to make sure that her kids won't be hungry. A person who provides her kids with supplies for home and school. A person who makes sure that her kids stay on top of school and make good grades and says I'm proud of you. A person who is raising her kids to be good adults and be successful in life. A person who works and comes home happy as ever. A person who makes sure that her bills are paid. A person who laughs and jokes around with her kids when we are together as family. A person who always tells me, If you want to be somebody you got to make that somebody come true. A person who keeps herself looking good every day, even when she comes home from work. A person who always says that boys isn't anything when it comes to your life. That person is Nicole Rice, a.k.a. my momma.

LaQuonn Williams

Grandma Love

Grandma love is like

you loving your best
song or movie or like

a hot sunny day or
finding a million dollars
or like falling in love with
someone, or like the best

day of your life, but grandma love
is not like any of those—
it is better.

Najae Jordan

Najae Jordan

Never giving up on anything I try
Always on top of my game
Just laid back and cool
Always has style and nice kicks
Exciting and willing to try new things

Joyful, fun and always making friends
Original but fly at the same time
Reaching my life goals
Daring to be a better person
Awesome at basketball and any other sport
Noticed for my hard work and good grades

I'Esha Davis

My Identity

What do I see when I look at myself
from 2nd grade until now...
I look back on my school year in 2nd grade. I look at
myself now and see the changes in me since I am much
older now.
I was really quiet.
Now I am outspoken.
The changes that I went through:
2nd grade, learning multiplication.
Now I am good at multiplication.
More overcome about how I choose my friends.
Hanging out with the right crowd of people.
Choosing my friends now that I am older.
Younger, maybe not telling the wrong people to stay
away and leave the crowd.
Just wanted some friends to be happy.
The changes that me and my friends came through.
Being fake,
Talking behind your back,
Starting fights with their friends and you,
They would make you get in trouble with your friends,
in life, and at school.
What if I thought about these changes in 2nd grade,
would I be a better person?

DaeJohn Wilson

Romance is a Killer, Romance is True Love

I am told...
Romance is a killer,
It has a lot of ups and downs,
They say xoxoxo to you,
He blows a kiss that same day.

What are these? They are not mine.
Shoes.
So whose are they?
Your birthday present.
I'm sorry honey, can you forgive me?
I thought you wanted chocolate & a candle dinner.
Where's the dinner?
It's at a special place. I know you like the 70's
so we are bringing them back.

Alexus Shockley

Am I a Brat?

I was always told I was spoiled by my aunt. They say I would go over to her house every weekend. When I went over there I would play and laugh but I would only cry when it was time for me to go home. When my mom came I would cry, scream, and have a big fit. But she would finally get me to come home and I would go back over there because I would play like I was sick. She would buy me anything I wanted even if it wasn't even my birthday, but she would make sure we were at church every Sunday.

My mom says I was spoiled then but she says I'm spoiled now and I say to myself, "I was spoiled ever since we moved into our new house." I think this brat thing is never going to come to an end because I can tell this story over and over again. Now I am thinking this is turning into a rhyme and now you might be thinking she is going to tell this story one more time. But in the end my friends say you might be spoiled and you need to break that shell. Then I say you are right because I can't get everything I want in life like show and tell.

I know you might think I'm going to be a brat all my life but you're wrong. I want to be a psychiatrist or maybe a nurse and help all the people I can because I am a helpful person and I will be the best I can!

Kamika Nelson

Friendship

All around me I saw no
friendship. I thought I could
have a friend to play with,
and go out and have fun. It took time
for me to be in a bestfriendrelationship.

One day I just thought I can talk to
someone and I got rejected. That made me
stop trying. A girl named Michelle
talked to me, and I was shocked and amazed
that someone talked to me.

Michelle and I got very close and did
what best friends do. In December she
asked me would I be her best friend. I said
I accept. We like to shop, talk on the phone,
and play around. What I like about her is
that she's country and her actions are funny.
What she likes about me is my style, and I
encourage her to do right and we party a lot.

What a friendship means to me is a
person who is honest, respectful, and
makes sure you're on the right track.

Darrien Daniels

Basketball

Ballers, something people can't notice
Athletics around the world
Best shooters in the country
Kings in B-Ball
Best talented players
Best jump-shots ever
Aggressive
Leaders in what we do
Intelligent ball players

Kenyatta Smith

My Favorite Uncle

The story about my favorite uncle is about my favorite
uncle doing things for us, about when my mom set
his hair on fire, and the last thing is about when he
was killed.

My mom used to always tell us the story of how
my uncle always used to be bad and how well they got
along sometimes. My mom had set my uncle's hair on
fire, because he had a lot of hair and he used to call
her bald-headed all the time. But my uncle did live
because it was just his hair. His hair was really uneven,
so he just cut it all off and had a low cut.

My uncle was my mom's youngest brother on my
grandmother's side. He did lots of things for the family.
He bought us things and spent a lot of time with us.
He used to plan our family reunions at the Lake of the
Ozarks for us and pay for our rooms, where we went
to stay for a day or two. My uncle was so nice that he
did anything we asked him to, like buy us things and
pay for our field trips. He was my favorite uncle in the
whole world.

After my uncle's death, the family was really sad
and was really mad at who did it and wanted to send
them to jail for a life penalty. My uncle's best friend
wanted to do the things my uncle did for us, because
he knew that my uncle was and still is very important
to us. My uncle's best friend was with my uncle when
he was killed on his motorcycle. My uncle's best

friend was paralyzed in his left arm, but he was sad that his best friend was gone too.

But to this day we still celebrate his birthday and go see him and do things that he liked to do for his birthday. We get a cake and party materials and we bar-beque and party until it is time to go home.

Deven Simms

My Friends

My friends are important to me because they help me with a lot, and also they are there for me. Duka and I have been friends since the fifth grade. Now we play on the same basketball and baseball team. We practice at the Wellston High School at 6:00 PM on Wednesday and Thursday. I have known Tommie my whole life. Growing up with Tommie, people told me about how bad he was. Tommie and I were on the same team at Central Elementary School. We always go to his house to play football on the PS2. Also we get chased every day before we get to his house. Thomas. I'm just now knowing him so we haven't done nothing yet, but played the game at his house. LeTrell, we just started hanging out. In the future we might split up, but I know we will still be friends.

DaeJohn Wilson

The Light

I see light, a very bright light.
It is a spspspspirit.
I wonder. I go closer and closer. It's moving.
I run and run.
I stop.
I wonder if I can catch it. I have a plan. I run back.
I start speeding. I stop.
BANG!
We crashed.
The spirit says, "Thanks for freeing me."
The light is dying.
I cry and say, "Goodbye, old friend."
I wonder whether I am in a new world.
I see a boy.
I ask, "Where Am I?"
He says in the middle of nowhere.
WHOOSH!
The boys says, "Follow me."
Alright.
He leads me to a time machine.
He asks, "Aren't you going to get in the time machine?"
Where will you go?
No.
As I get in the time machine I say my final goodbye.

Jamie Davis

Who Am I?

Short,
African American,
and talented.
Positive parts of me.
But most of all
What is there to know
about me?
I think so hard,
but can never figure out
who I am.
Who am I? Who am I? Who am I?
Asking myself everyday.
When I get frustrated about myself,
I cry.
Crying this nonsense away.
My tears are like hail,
Falling from a flaming red sky.

I pray for God,
hope that he would lead me the way.
Wondering…
Why he never answers.
It hurts me so much.
But most of all

he wants me to be,
only who I am.

Jubilant,
Anxious,
and mysterious
is who I am.
I'm proud
of who I was born to be.

Born a child,
the best part of me.
It's who and what
I was born to be.
My identity…
is who I am,
not who I am not.

Kathon Robinson

I Remember

I remember my aunt told me
Never to do drugs.

She was dark-skinned,
Medium height,
Low-cut hair,
Always had a new gold tooth,
And always sat with her back straight up.

I remember having parties
When she was sitting in the kitchen
Sipping on some wine cooler.
She used to love going to bingo
On the weekends.

I remember every time she left
She told me
She will be right back
And she came back.

Before she went up
She told me
See you later.

It was after school when I found out.
My heart was so broken up.

She was the best aunt of all.
I really love her.
Right after the funeral I was
Singing a song for her,
Saying
It's so hard to say goodbye to yesterday,

Face full of tears
Wishing she was here.

And now I know
She will never be back again.
She passed on my sister's birthday.

But until it's my time
To come up
I will always remember
Having parties, dancing,
Singing, having dinner,
And joking around.

Brandi George

"Me"

See I live in Wellston which is a bad neighborhood,
we're going to live in a town house I think we should.

See I watch Bloods and Crips, the next thing I know
they going to be talking 'bout R.I.P.

People out here getting shot and killed, teachers be mad
at us 'cause Wellston don't pay their bills.

That's my life with good looking and pain, sometimes
I also say this life, this school, these people is a shame.

Jevon Cannon

The Streets

People trying to make a living
Struggle and starve
Making their way to feed their kids
Making way for them to live
Hoping they will have a better life than this
Doing drugs that's the way she lives
Not caring for her kids
Thinking drugs will stop the pain
All it is doing is destroying her brain
Not thinking right opening her legs day and night
Opening her legs thinking that's the way she must eat
Good potential going to waste ask yourself
How long it's going to take
Until her body is going to break

Darrion Stinson

Walking to the Death

Walking to the Death
of a Dad

Walking to the Death
of a Mom

Walking to the Death
of a Son

Walking to the Death
of a Daughter

See that family the Death of that family.

Thomas Jackson

Thank You All

Thank you for
Helping me
Obey the people in my life because if I didn't there
    would be all sorts of
Madness in my future
All because I didn't control my attitude everywhere I
    went even in
School

Just letting you
All know that I, Thomas Jackson, have good
Character in everything I do even in different
Kinds of
Sports
Overcoming
New things in my life

Michelle Stokes

Sing

Singing is my life. When I feel down
All I have to do is sing.
When I sing it makes all my dreams
come true.

In my life it may be hard but I make it
So when it seems hard it's not.
When people hear me sing they say, "Wow that's
hot!" But in my life, some people think
I'm nobody, but they're wrong.

My mom always said that life is like a war.
You have to fight for it and that's what I do
For singing.
I love to sing, you see, if I have to go over
The ocean I will. And that's how bad I love to
sing.

So when you see me on t.v., you will say
that I did what I wanted to do with
My life and you will get my CD.

And for all the people that hated me
that's what made me do it even harder,
That's why my song is hot and
that's why I made it.

Clockwise from top right:
DuShai Jackson,
Tinisha Hardwrict,
Alexis Cole,
Jevon Cannon,
Michelle Stokes

Clockwise from top right:
LaQuonn Williams,
De'Carla Latchison,
Darrion Stinson,
Perry Green,
Darrien Daniels

Clockwise from top right:
LeTrell Crews,
Tommie Wilson,
Kevin McLemore,
Deven Simms,
Adam Moore

Clockwise from top:
Cameshia Mays,
Brandi George,
Najae Jordan,
Roderick Reed,
Alexus Shockley

Clockwise from top:
Cushure Hall,
Tanzania Taylor,
Jamonica Gallion,
Thomas Jackson,
Shanika Price

Clockwise from top:
Deyon Smith,
Jason Vasser,
Jamie Davis,
I'Esha Davis,
DaeJohn Wilson

Clockwise from top:
Antonio Pulliam,
James Bush,
Tess Thompson,
Kenyatta Smith,
K. Curtis Lyle

Clockwise from *top*:
Kathon Robinson,
Dasia Rice,
Matt Picard,
Robin Edwards

Cameshia Mays

The Elegant Angels

I like to dance. I love to dance because I get to show a lot of my family and friends, and also I can perform in front of people.

I really like to dance to hip hop music and sometimes slow and fast gospel music. Sometimes when I dance I am shy in front of people but when I dance I just let it flow and I don't be scared or nervous anymore.

I remember one time I was at church and I and my dance team had made up a dance to do for the church. So one Sunday we did the dance and it was like a hip-hop gospel dance.

I was really excited because it was like my first performance in front of a lot of people. But after then I just was dancing in front of everybody and not being scared.

My dance team, which was called "The Elegant Angels," all had on the same thing which was blue jeans, red and black shirts that had words on them, and jackets that had our dance name on the back, and my dance name was Faith. The music had a hip hop beat but it was gospel words and the gospel words was like, Represent get crunk, represent get crunk if you know you reppin' Jesus go on 'head and throw it up.

Perry Green

My Poems

My poems are always
about love, family, friendship, and life.
This is how I grow in my life.
Me and my five cousins did a lot
with each other.
We played all type of games and sports
like basketball and football.
We had always went to the mall
with each other.
We always had each other's back.
Everybody always tells me that I'm growing up
to be a young man.
All my teachers tell me that I am a successful person.
I try to do things
that people never think of.
I always wanted my
drawings to be big 'cause
I always think of new Ideas. Me, myself,
Perry will grow up and be the most
successful person my family knows.

De'Carla Latchison

How My Life Has Been Since I Got Older

I remember I was so flexible.
I could've put both of my legs
behind my head. Now I can put
one leg behind my head then do a split.
I used to be a sweet angel.
I don't know what happened.
Did bad boys and girls influence me?
Did I change my ways to be like a clown?

No! It was me who changed me.
I am a brilliant 13-year-old girl.
I am an intelligent young scholar.
I am a beautiful, unique, and determined girl.
I am like a rock.
I am like a rock because when someone
in my class is doing something bad.
I do something good so they can see that I'm
being a rock they can be a rock too.

Tommie Wilson

What I Want To Be

Like 10 years from now I will like to be a police officer because my Uncle Rat is a police officer and I want to feel the pain that they're feeling right now. They got to put up the bad people from selling drugs on the street and stop people from killing each other.

I want to feel like putting on a badge and going after the bad people and chasing cars running from the law. If they get away I will find them and it will look ugly. How I feel about being a police is great, smart, and fun. It will make the city look better than it was and get all the drugs off the street.

Tinisha Hardwrict

JuDgE mE

Judge me how you want to
but one thing I know is that I'm beautiful
You can call me black, ugly, dumb, or even crazy.
But I know I'm a black African American
I don't care what you think of me,
I know who I am and how I look.
I didn't come in this world to be liked or to be perfect.
Once somebody told me I was dumb. I use that word as
a motivation
to take me farther in life and to trust myself
I need to stop and prove that person wrong
make a believer out of him.
I would not let him know that he's right
I have to focus on my life, nobody else.
I was taught everywhere you go
you will always have haters or somebody
talking about you.
I used to look at myself in the mirror like, you is dumb.
But I can't listen to him because he wants to see me
down while
I got family and friends that want to see me up.

Talent
Intelligent
Nice
Independent
Shy
High-Esteem
Amazing

Shanika Price

Who Am I?

Who am I, I am
I am a girl that has fun
And that's me, Shanika.

And I am a girl that
Loves to jump rope and play games.
Is this me, is it?

I know that I like
To play with my friends and with
My family too

And sometime I like
To play on the computer
And also, I am

A big sister that
Loves and cares for them, that's me
This is me, it is!

Alexis Cole

Who Am I?

A beautiful black girl.
My hair sandy brown
like honey and long
like ocean waves.

My smile
gives me confidence.
And courage to know what to do
when I'm disappointed.
My body turns
my smile
around to be the prettiest
smile in the nation.

My hands
as I pick up a pen
and write ideas.
My phalanges
as I scoop up a book
and read
it full of knowledge
and education.

My feet
as I learn
the dance steps
so I can perform
enormous shows.

My eyes
dark brown
like the root of a tree
that lets me see
my future.

My skin
as antique
vanilla, like Prairie Farm
ice cream
smooth, soft and sensitive.

My personality
as a smart and brilliant
person who likes to joke around
and still work hard
to make the outstanding and significant
grades that I get.

Aeriona Watts

A Person with Bright Ideas

Awesome in many ways, seeking out to find who
    I can be.
Eager to learn more about the world so that I
    can be
Ready to put on my thinking cap to do many brand
    new
Intelligent things with what is offered to me so
    that I can create an
Outstanding piece that will be honored and well
    respected as it is read.
Now knowing that someone has gotten a chance
    to be inspired by me makes me proud
And makes my family happy; they know that I
    can do it.

Robin Edwards

Memories

I remember when I was eight.
I used to watch T.V. and stay up late.
I remember when I was nine.
I always wished that I could fly.

I remember when I was ten.
I would count to ten over and over again.
I remember when I was eleven.
I prayed and prayed to go to heaven.

I remember when I was twelve.
I really liked Tinker Bell.
I am thirteen and pretty as can be.
The best age to remember is when I was three.
I used to run around and be free.
I yelled and screamed and climbed on everything.

I ate with my fingers and started fights with my
little sister.
Being three was best for me.

LeTrell Crews

Trip to California

When I went to California I thought that it was going to get dark fast just like St. Louis but it didn't. It seemed like it was taking a long time to get dark. But St. Louis time is just faster than California. Their air is not bad. The food smelled good and tasted good. I saw some monkeys. That was very cool.

When I got used to it, I started to make some friends. When we lived in Apple Valley, we met a lot of friends and we went to school together. I was trying to play football but my mom couldn't find a team for my brother and me, so we just were going to the park and playing basketball. We used to go rock climbing every day. Sometimes we heard dogs at night time. One day when I climbed a mountain, I saw a dog and then we started to run down the hill so fast, so we wouldn't get bitten.

Adayshia Jackson

Myself, Generation to My Black History

My name it's more different but
my traits are quite the same.
My generation it goes on to
where my grandmom can't explain.
My history is a long story
my grandfather keeps on complaining
saying he won't tell
there was a struggle back in the day
people were being lynched just for
the color of the skin.
But the way I see it, we're all the same,
color just don't blend.
Our colors may be different but
we have the blood and the
same voice of opinion.

I'm 12 years of age.
I have 6 sisters in my life.
It's not perfect, but
I'm glad to be living.
My mom is always saying life is not perfect.
I understand what she's saying but I
don't want to listen because to me it could
be better.
Life is a big struggle

trying to survive.
To me it's a big ball
trying to explode.
My family it's a nice size
but it shortens by the days
because life, it's too short.
So don't take life for granted.
Live it like it's your only life.

Jamie Davis

Miracle

A special child.
The age of seven.
A miracle to me.
I thought I was dreaming.
because he
was still with me.

A miracle…
Shaking unbelievably,
I was scared to see
I believe it was a seizure
Very hard for me

What a miracle…

I called the police,
Anxiously and scared.
He was rushed to the hospital
Young and helpless

Still a miracle…

Right out of the blue,
Here come two more seizures
Even scarier than the first one
Two to four days in the hospital
I couldn't bear it anymore.

Hope for a miracle…

I thought
He was going to leave me
Like my beloved birds that were
Buried under me.
Not able to spread his wings
And become a great man.
Cried for days
Until he was back in my hands.

The miracle that saved a boy close to me.

Darrion Stinson

Grandma

Grandma – You know me so well
Grandma – You know me so well
Grandma – You know me so well

There's only one lady that knows me well,
That well to tell. What?
Anyone that I can tell, she knows me very well.
If people don't know me that well,
She can tell just because she knows me so well.
That doesn't mean I can tell that you know me
Very well.

Sometimes I know Hell, but you know it
Well that all I know is Heaven
Because when you are in it, you can tell you know
Heaven so well.

This is the part I can tell,
My dad, I know well, my mom, getting well…
My family I know very well. We've been around a very
Long time, Halloween, Christmas, Easter, Thanksgiving
And out to eat, bowling and skating parties.

My Grandma is the first one I lived with.
When my dad was little, my Grandma
Whooped him with a switch
Plenty of times, but when she died
The Devil lied and said that she was going to go
Down There with him, instead, she
Went to Heaven.
Two years ago my grandma died, we
Cried, cried, and cried. Then, from time to
Time we still cried. Now we go to her grave because
We miss her and
She still didn't forget that she knows me so well.

I'Esha Davis

A Great Friend

A great friend would tell you the truth about what they
did or how they did it.
You would know more things about your friends than
their enemies or people that they don't like or had a
bad memory with.

A great friend would have high self-esteem.
Your friend would think they are as intelligent and
honest and not see anything wrong with their life or
personality.

A great friend would tell you everything, whether it is
good or bad.
Your friend would tell you things that they did that they
would not tell their parents or other family members.

A great friend would have your back no matter what
you are going through.
Tell you to keep your thoughts clear and be truthful and
not useful. Try to keep you happy instead of sad.

A great friend would help you through a bad family
situation.

A great friend would help you choose the right friends
when your friends are not helpful.
Tell you to stop hanging out with a person that has a
dangerous or bad background.

A great friend would not try to hurt you.
Your friend would not fight you and keep you feeling down.

My friends are faithful to me and keep me having fun and lots of energy.
How would your friends handle the situation?

Kevin McLemore

The Energetic Boy

Man, man, man. This boy Lil Rell, that's his name, he has all the energy in him. I remember one time he helped me when I fell off a four-wheeler because it was too fast for me. I love this boy.

I love this boy. Lil Rell likes to jump around, loves to play, loves to drive four-wheelers, play basketball, football, and baseball. I love this boy.

I love this boy. I love him because he helps me and he's kind. Energy energy energy everywhere in his body. I wish I had energy in my body. I love this boy.

I love this boy. I love him because you're supposed to love your family, because if you love them, they are going to love you back, or do something nice for you. I love this boy.

I love this boy. When I'm around him I feel so excited because he's the best best best energetic boy cousin I ever had. I love this boy.

Cushsure Hall

Who am I?

who am I, who am I?
am I just a regular boy?
I don't know.
who am I, who am I?
are me and you the same?
who am I, who am I?
another African American?
who am I, who am I?
just a boy named Cushsure Hall?

No!!!!!!!
I know who I am
a strong African American
with lots of pride
I am not like you
I am unique in my own ways
you don't know me
I don't know me
but one day
I will figure out who I am.

Jamonica Gallion

Memories of Constance Jefferson

I remember my granny with love. My granny was a
real short lady. She had a lot of gray hair, and she was
72 years old. Even though she is in heaven I still think
about her. I still have enough room in my heart for her
and my momma.

My granny had nine kids. My mom, my sister, and
I used to go over to my granny and granddaddy's house
when my lil sister got out of school. We used to sit
down in her living room and watch Lifetime together.
My granny used to set a bowl of candy on the table for
all her grandkids. My granny's favorite color was pink.
She used to have a lot of perfume. Her favorite was
White Diamond. She used to know how to cook and
she showed all of her nine kids how to cook. Any time
somebody cooked in our family my granny would go
home from church and change clothes so she could go
eat.

My granny was really special to me. My granny
loved to go to church with her husband. My granddaddy's father died. Now the only person my granddaddy
has is his mother.

DuShai Jackson

Life

Life, what does it mean,
Life is just a word, or is it?
Let me tell you about Life,

It begins when your mom gave birth,
When you were blessed by the Lord at church,
To be his child in this world and the next,
You let yourself be known,
To the day you would finally be gone,

Life is a mystery,
Life is suspicious,
It can be ridiculous,
But all you need to do is live it to its fullest.

Love
Intelligence
Fun
Exciting

Roderick Reed

My Great Grandma

I loved her like I never loved anyone before. She was my heart and my soul. My great grandma was always thinking about me. She would try to break her back to give me a dollar. My great grandma wasn't supposed to smoke, but she would sneak and smoke anyway. Then she passed December 28, 2006, the worst day of my life.

My great grandma was a great card player. She taught our whole family how to play. The kinds of cards she liked playing were tunk, spades, and gin rummy. She would always want us to go to the store for her.

My great grandma was a strong woman. She had twelve kids and six preceded her in death. She was a beautiful woman and a good dresser. She was very stylish. She was short with black pretty hair. She always loved those business suits in all different colors. She always had a stylish hair-do with bangs and curls. Some of her suits were red, white, blue, and more.

My great grandma treated everybody like her own. She was a great woman. My great grandma would be still living but her daughters didn't want her living on a breathing machine. She smoked her whole life. That is what made her sick. When she was sick in the hospital, she was very swollen. When some kids used to treat her bad, those were the ones who took it the worst when she died. Her funeral was very beautiful but we don't have enough money to get her a headstone so she doesn't have a headstone yet.

Deyon Smith

Life

Life is like a cat it sneaks up on you
Life teaches you that losing something can be gaining
something more,

Life is like a zoo it's filled with new things,
Life teaches you to be smart,

Life is like a whirlwind and goes around and around
Life teaches you to be brave,

Life is like a kid at school
who learns a lot,

Life isn't just a game
life isn't hard
life isn't about me or you,

life is just life...

life is crazy
life is long
life is all alone,

life is just life...

Life... Life... Life...

Tanzania Taylor

What I Do Haikus

Hey, what do I do?
I like to jump rope a lot
and talk on the phone

What else do I do?
I also like to crack jokes
to family and friends.

What else do I do?
Love to eat and watch t.v.
Such as watch Sponge Bob

What else do I do?
I love going to the mall
With my nice, cool friends.

What else do I do?
I just love doing cool things.
These things equal me!

James Bush

Heart in Soul

Heart in Soul, Heart in Soul
Let your heart be in your soul

Let bad things out and good things in

Don't drink gin
Gin is bad
Not like Ben
Ben is glad

People die every day
But God let me be here today

Thank you, thank you, thank you God

I'm glad to be me
and hope and wish to be
You let me live to the end of the day
Let us see your face, OK?

Antonio Pulliam

The Line Of Scrimmage

When I get dat feel,
of being on da field,
it ain't no time ta yield.
I'm going at my own speed,
You gon have injuries,
You gon bleed,
If you're on da other side of da line,
You betta hide,
You betta run,
Cuz I'm coming faster than a bullet from a gun,
I can't breathe,
I need air ta fill my lungs,
Because that's how hard I play,
I'm going to take drastic measures to make you lay
I'm gon hit ya harder than a AK.
I talk a lot of trash but you ain't listening to what I say,
Cuz I back mines up,
When the Quarterback puts his signs up,
He betta motion because I'm slicker than lotion,
I can't explain my devotion,
I'm listening when the boss is coaching,
You ain't nothing to me you a pest, a rodent,
The scent of the grass is so potent,
Remember me,
NOT now,
NOT later,
FOREVER.

Adam Moore

I Remember the Pain

I remember the pain. Below my waist blood ran down as if it was paint. I could see where it was broken because the bone was almost showing. Memories flashed as if I was going to die. I felt so light-headed I thought I could fly. Why did I climb on top of the garage? When I hit the ground I saw a mirage. It looked like a tall man standing over me with a long jacket on and he had on a big hat.

When I came back to my senses it was my big brother trying to pick me up. We were making a club-house out of a garage that was abandoned. I was trying to cover the hole in the roof that the rain was making. I was holding on to a broken-off brick. I was getting ready to climb off and one of the bricks I was holding on to fell and so did two or three bricks that were connected to that one.

Three to four bricks were on my leg. I was lucky that none was on my head. My big brother and my friend helped me home. My mama was scared because she saw all of that blood. They ripped my pants and washed all the blood off my leg.

I went to the doctor and got X-rays. The doctor said I was lucky I didn't fall on my neck. They gave me a cast, which I had for a month and seven days. When I got home and everybody saw I was ok they teased me about how I was crying. I remember the pain.

De'Carla Latchison

Music

When I feel life is ever so painful
I put on my headphones
Block out the world's madness
And let it drift me away.

These lyrics
These beats
Become a part of me
It becomes my hope for peace.

One beat two beat
It becomes the beat of my heart.
My heart beats faster.
And I begin to close my eyes.

I let it drift me away.
I want to be free.
I want to free my soul.
I want to get lost within these beats.

I stop the music.
Look around me
The world hasn't changed.
I hit the play button once again.

Kaimen Pascall

I Remember

I remember when I heard it. I remember that day I was about two years old. I remember it made my body cold. I remember I shook. I remember I looked for it. I had to look. I remember when I found it. It changed my life. It's what keeps me going. It's what keeps my blood flowing. In the morning when God wakes me up, I remember music. Music made me, it molded me, music will never go old. I remember every day, music gave me rhythm. I remember music is why I'm living. I remember what kind I like, rap, rock, anything. As long as it's about music, I'll listen to anything.

Tinesha McLemore

Beautiful Me

Me, me, me people think I'm all about myself
    'cause I'm beautiful.
The light shines on me when I'm on stage or outside
    walking down the street,
and people see how beautiful I am.
They should just see right through me and know
    under that beautiful skin
there is something beautiful and special, more than
    just myself.
Intelligent mind, smart thinking young lady, and I am
    extremely fun at times.
I get good grades in school. I try my best to work hard
    during my class periods.
With friends, family, and people, I am surrounded by
    people I love.
I'm not about myself, I'm about other people too.
I tell people they look good when they wear
    something nice,
when they get their hair done, or look nice on
    a sunny day
or when their cheeks turn red from the cold.
You see, you see it's not about just me. It's about the
    world you see.
People around the world that are intelligent have things
    in common, and beauty is one of them.

Najae Jordan

Dark Empty Room

spacious, empty, one
big black box

lonely quiet scared as
four walls surround me
as quiet sounds loud

nowhere to go.
nowhere to hide.
no one but me.

but wait,
as I slide along the
four smooth walls
I feel something cold
and round

I think it's a doorknob
I'm not sure, maybe
there's hope,
hope for freedom

Alexus Shockley

A Child of Why

As I was growing I wasn't a child of how,
I was a child of why.
I was not the type of child who asked questions,
like how does that work?
How did you pass that test?
Most people want to know how
but they should be asking why.

I asked questions like
Why am I so concerned in my work?
Why do I go to school?
Why do I have friends?
Why do people fight?
Why do I ask questions?

Now I am older I can stop asking why
when I ask questions
and answer them.

StudioSTL

StudioSTL has been around since May 2005 when seven strangers first met to discuss the possibility of developing a community writing center based on a successful San Francisco model founded by author Dave Eggers called, "826 Valencia." The group shared a mutual passion for writing, for the power and potential of young minds, for teachers, for creativity and excellence and for the fair city of St. Louis. Many meetings later, the group (no longer strangers) unanimously agreed to pour their hearts, souls and brainpower into building a magical, one-of-a-kind, drop-in writing center.

We're moving forward! Imagine seven-year olds penning stories for a miniature dachshund named Haley, or sixth-graders becoming members of an international press corps with a once-in-lifetime chance to interview the slightly odd and widely unknown, "Sir J.T. Scowling" – an author who, much to the kids' surprise happens to suffer from writer's block? Think of a poet, writer, AP reporter and illustrator working with thoughts and ideas in front of 250 eighth-graders!

The acclaimed StudioSTL anthology series debuted last June with publication of StudioSTL Number 1: self-portraits written by the students of College Bound. In a Foreword, St. Louis Rams wide-receiver Isaac Bruce wrote: "It's filled with wisdom from high school students who were faster than I was when it comes to getting a leg up on life." We offer our anthology series for sale at local retailers (and nationally) to help fund our free writing services and other student publishing projects.

We now have three student press corps with journalists who fan out across the city donned with press passes and notebooks to get "the scoop" from town notables and superstars, including Senator Jean Carnahan, Circuit Attorney Jennifer Joyce, Mizzou football star Jeremy Maclin and a host of other do-gooders who share everything, from cupcakes to soul food. The self-titled "Tall Tale Truth" will publish a third issue in the summer 2008, and StudioSTL will publish additional cutting edge news and features written by members of our Freedom School and Twenty-First Century Press Corps.

To round out our student publications, StudioSTL offers a one-of-a-kind student literary magazine. Every Saturday morning in the fall and spring, young minds gather with give-back, can-do mentoring teams from the Saint Louis University Undergraduate English Club. We call it a donut-eating, guitar-strumming, creative haven for curious, out-of-the-box thinkers. The result is a compilation of poetry, cartoons, fiction, and song-writing from some of the most creative young minds in St. Louis.

We're in schools. We're mentoring. We're working on more student publications. And we're downright thrilled at the opportunity to share the power and magic of words.

The Wellston Project

In acknowledging all of those whose combined efforts brought this project to fruition, I would like to first recognize the students, for it is they who have taken the great risk here. Putting pen to paper with creativity and passion is a rarity in today's educational culture of standards and measured objectives. No rubric can quantify the courage necessary to sit down and commit oneself to sincere expression or the joy borne out succeeding in its pursuit. Many of the students asked of themselves during this process, "Who am I?" In response, I'd say you are writers. And I am proud of you.

Next, it is only appropriate to give credit, a hearty and generous helping of it, to StudioSTL—Beth Ketcher, Jason Nicholas Vasser, Tess Thompson, the pioneering students of the College Bound anthology, and all of the thoughtful and dedicated mentors whose varied backgrounds in writing and living inspired the students and breathed life into our Thursday workshops. It was you who provided the platform from which the students leapt headlong into writing as they never had before, and it was you who caught them when they fell upon frustration or self-doubt. Thank you for your willingness to be as vulnerable as the students in sharing your own visions and processes.

Finally, I would be remiss if I did not give credit to those who strive daily to provide the students with the support, encouragement, and academic skills essential to continuing the exercise of self-inquiry beyond this singular triumph. This includes our administrators, Ms. Stewart and Ms. Reid, as well as all of the teachers and staff of Curtis Bishop Middle School. For it is on their shoulders that the students of this anthology will stand, facing a future of truth, hope, and happiness.

Matt Picard
7th Grade English Teacher
Bishop Middle School

When I first entered Matt Picard's classroom at Bishop Middle School, I wanted to stay awhile. He had made a cozy reading and writing nook in the corner by bringing in lap desks and a secondhand couch. The walls were adorned with pictures of writers and inspirational quotations about writing. His students, already accustomed to honing their work in writing workshops, had already met some of the high school students published in the first StudioSTL anthology, and they were ready to get to work on a book of their own. We came into the classroom weekly in February and March to work with them on telling their own stories.

Having worked on several StudioSTL projects, I can say that one of the strengths of the organization is bringing together people in the St. Louis area from many walks of life. Our mentors ranged from college students to a professional writer with a Ph.D. and many years' experience. It was a delight to exchange ideas with the mentors and my co-director as we worked together to highlight these middle school students' words. I am grateful to the students for accepting us into their classroom and trusting us to listen to what they had to say. Their work is filled with emotional honesty, and I am proud to see them share it with the St. Louis community.

Tess Thompson
Writer

All too often within the African American community we hear stories of the violence the young inflict upon themselves and the people around them. One may even hear on the news about how a local gang member committed a crime or how a couple of children got escorted off school premises for fighting, though through all of the issues that our community faces everyday, children make the most change. It is my belief that there is an innocence in the youth that reaches out for help, but those cries often fall on deaf ears. It was an extreme pleasure to work with the seventh grade class at Bishop Middle School because they were so eager to learn and were not afraid to be vulnerable in the act of expressing themselves. This particular group of children shared with me their story: one of struggle, one of triumph, one of life.

I think that it is necessary for the world to see that these young middle school students are not all running the streets, but away from them. I want the community to realize that these young African American youths have something they are trying to say. It is not their fault that they have to fear for their lives more often then we think. This world forces them to be hard. It's difficult, and life for the people in our community has never been easy. Through the arts we overcome, through the arts we are able to cope, and it is through the arts that the world can see the light within us shine bright. I feel honored that I was able to work with these future leaders of our world, and I am proud of who they are. I can't wait for the world to see them for who they are as well.

Jason Nicholas Vasser
Poet

Contributor Notes & Acknowledgments

JAMES BUSH would like to thank his mom for helping him get through school, his dad for helping him too, and his family for keeping him out of trouble. And last, but not least, he would like to thank his big brothers for teaching him a lot in life. He would also like to thank StudioSTL.

JEVON CANNON says, "To me, poems, one of a kind. Certain people, it's a crime. But to me, it's my way to shine." Jevon likes playing sports, hanging with friends, and playing games. He says he gets his knowledge from his elders, which helps him walk the streets and reminds him of all things good and bad before he gets into trouble.

ALEXIS COLE says she is a beautiful black girl who loves to cheer, dance and sing. She liked how the StudioSTL mentors helped her with her writing and corrected her work. She says StudioSTL inspired her to get into writing poetry and other types of writing.

LETRELL CREWS was born in St. Louis and lived here until he was nine years old, and then he moved to California for two years. He now lives in St. Louis with four brothers and one sister. He believes that writing is a great thing to do and is the best thing you can do in your life.

DARRIEN DANIELS loves to write and read, and he says that StudioSTL was the best thing going for him on Thursdays. He likes to write about things or about himself. He gets a pen or pencil and just gets to writing.

I'ESHA DAVIS thinks writing is important because she can put down anything she wants to and describe things that go on in her life. She loves her family and friends.

JAMIE DAVIS is part of a big family. She loves writing because she can write down what she's feeling, and when she's with her siblings, she writes a lot. The most important thing she likes about writing is that no one can judge her or what she is saying.

ROBIN EDWARDS says that she is a talented, black African-American girl, 5'4" tall, who loves to talk. Her favorite television show is "Degrassi," and her favorite foods are chicken and french fries. Her favorite types of music are Hip Hop and R&B, and her favorite song is "Get Silly."

JAMONICA GALLION likes to jump rope, play basketball, go shopping, and party. When she is home she likes to talk on the phone and watch TV. She will enjoy being in a book. She really liked freewriting and having the writers read their lovely poetry. Most of all, she really enjoyed StudioSTL coming to her school and spending all fifty minutes with her class.

BRANDI GEORGE lives in Wellston and loves basketball. When she grows up, she wants to be in the Women's

National Basketball Association. At Bishop, she likes health class and gym.

PERRY GREEN likes to go to his grandma's house and have fun. He likes writing because he can express his feelings.

CUSHSURE HALL likes to play sports: basketball, football, tennis. He never gives up. He would like to thank StudioSTL for this opportunity. He wants to give a shout-out to his family: "I love you."

TINISHA HARDWRICT would like thank StudioSTL for coming in and working with the Wellston students. She would also like to thank her granny and her mother for taking time out of their lives to care for her. She would also like to thank Mr. Picard, her Language Arts teacher, for being there for her and the other students when they need him.

DUSHAI JACKSON was born in St. Louis and has been here from past to present. He has a lot of memories with his family (two brothers, one sister, mom, dad, and grandma). He says StudioSTL has helped him become a better person because he can put his thoughts on paper and express what he is feeling. This program has helped him become a better writer, let him express himself, and let him understand what's precious in life. Writing on paper helps him reveal his feelings.

THOMAS JACKSON didn't know how to write acrostic poems before StudioSTL came to his class. He says now he has learned to write all different kinds of poems.

NAJAE JORDAN likes to play basketball and a lot of other sports. She wrote her poem because she wants people to know who she is: a cool and a nice person. She's Najae Jordan.

DE'CARLA LATCHISON grew up in Wellston with her family and friends. She learned a lot during this program and it helped her with her writing skills. She learned how to write haiku, acrostics, and poems about herself. This program helped her because she was struggling with writing and it helped her go deeper than she thought she could.

CAMESHIA MAYS likes to play sports and jump doubledutch. She thanks her mom because if it wasn't for her, she wouldn't be here to talk or hear about StudioSTL. She wants to thank StudioSTL for coming to share with the class and for giving them the opportunity to be in a book.

KEVIN MCLEMORE likes this project and StudioSTL because he got the chance to do a lot of fun things, such as writing poems and hearing Mr. Nicholas read his poems. He thinks StudioSTL is tight because they are going to put the poems and pictures in a book.

ADAM MOORE believes that school is one of the most important things in his life because without it you couldn't really do anything and you would have to do things that are illegal to provide for your family. He would rather stay in school than take a chance of being in prison.

SHANIKA PRICE wants to thank her mom because she is happy with anything Shanika does and because she loves her too. She also wants to thank her family, friends, and StudioSTL because they have helped her find out who she is.

ANTONIO PULLIAM wants to thank his granddad, StudioSTL, and his family. He says that his poem in this book is possible because of his rapping and football abilities. He wants to thank Mr. Nicholas for opening his skills to the paper; without him, he probably would not have written his poem.

RODERICK REED grew up in Wellston with his mom, three brothers, and one sister.

DASIA RICE likes hanging out with friends who are real and who understand her. She likes dancing with her friends and just being herself. She says she is a very lovely person who hates saying "no" to people. She would like to thank StudioSTL for everything they've done and her momma for everything.

KATHON ROBINSON says that although he wasn't in class for all the writing sessions, when he was there, he really enjoyed it. Until StudioSTL came along, he didn't really like reading programs. Now he really likes it. Since this program, he has written three more things: about football, life, and who he is. He plans on writing poetry when he feels mad, and he wants to thank StudioSTL.

ALEXUS SHOCKLEY would like to thank StudioSTL for coming to take the time to show her class how to become little writers. She would also like to thank the StudioSTL writers for encouraging her to do and try her best at all times. She likes to hang out with her friends, talk on the phone, and just sit back and be herself. She wants to finish school and become a psychiatrist.

DEVEN SIMMS likes sports and wants to be a baseball or basketball player. He grew up on Wellsmar in Wellston with eight other family members.

DEYON SMITH wants to thank his mom for giving him a chance to be here and have this opportunity to write his poem. He wants to say thank StudioSTL for the chance to do this.

KENYATTA SMITH would like to be a veterinarian when she gets older because she enjoys taking good care of the animals and making sure that they are ready to go home or to a new home. She thinks that she would like to be a veterinarian because she loves animals.

DARRION STINSON is a twelve-year old boy that does not do anything, but really likes to play baseball, football, kickball, dodge ball, and lots of other sports. He likes writing a poem and putting it in a book. He says he never thought anybody would do that for him.

MICHELLE STOKES says that it's hard to be who she is and that sometimes she gets so weak she can't even speak. Her mom says, "Michelle, you is you." She knows that nobody can change her and that this is who she is.

TANZANIA TAYLOR likes playing jump rope, swimming, and talking on the phone with her friends. She enjoyed this program because it gave her and her classmates a chance to talk about themselves and show their skills.

LAQUONN WILLIAMS loves to play games, and he would love to become a real-estate agent. He likes to play basketball and ride his bike. Through this program, he learned how to write a better poem.

DAEJOHN "DJ" WILSON likes writing because he can freewrite and put his feelings on paper. When a teacher makes him mad, he can write his feelings down, or he can write to describe games he likes.

TOMMIE WILSON likes to play football and run track. He wants to be a police officer or a professional football player.

K. Curtis Lyle

K. CURTIS LYLE was born and raised in Los Angeles,
California. He was a founding member of the Watts
Writers Workshop, joining it in 1966 and becoming
a prominent member of the Los Angeles renaissance,
which the group represented. He has taught, lectured,
and read his poetry in performance in the major intel-
lectual and urban centers of North America. Lyle is
committed to restoring poetry to the forefront of performing and ritual arts. He currently lives in St. Louis,
Missouri where is an award-winning culture critic
for the St. Louis American, a weekly African American
newspaper.

Mentors

*Volunteer writing mentors play a crucial role in StudioSTL projects.
Five mentors worked with the students on the writing in this
anthology.*

BETTY BURNETT, Ph.D., is the author of several histori-
cal works. Her latest book is *St. Louis Yesterday and Today*, an
illustrated popular history of the city.

RAE DRAIZEN is a StudioSTL intern from Oakland,
California. She is currently a sophomore at Washington
University in St. Louis, majoring in Urban Studies and
Educational Studies. Working on this anthology has
been a dream come true, and she would like to thank
everyone involved!

EMMA JEHLE is an undergraduate at Saint Louis University pursuing degrees in French and International Studies. She grew up in St. Charles with her parents and seven sisters. After graduating, she hopes to be a part of Teach For America and plans on pursuing a career in education.

JEANNE SABBERT SMITH is an explorer of worlds both real and imagined. She has journeyed through childhood and adolescence with her son, Zach, and her daughter, Lydia. She discovers new points of view daily with her philosophy students at St. Louis University. Her traveling companion for the past 24 years is her husband Jim, who shares her passion for StudioSTL.

BRADEN WELBORN is a native of Birmingham, Alabama. Her poetry has appeared in *Prairie Schooner*, *Georgetown Review*, and *Crab Orchard Review*. She earned an M.F.A. in Creative Writing at the University of Alabama and an M.A. in Literature at Washington University in St. Louis.

Co-Directors

The project was led by two co-directors.

TESS THOMPSON has a master's degree in Literature from Oxford University and a B.A. in English from Penn State. A former high school teacher, she has published fiction in *Seventeen* and *Rosebud*. Her poetry has appeared in *Calyx*, *Literary Mama*, *ByLine*, *Tempus*, and *Philadelphia Stories*.

JASON NICHOLAS VASSER stumbled into the world on a windy October morning, full of the love given him by his parents. It wasn't until middle school that he came into loving the art of writing, reading, and reciting poetry at Visual Performing Arts at Marquette Middle School. Since then he has been published in *Today in Church* magazine as their premier poet, a local youth magazine called *Sisters and Guys (SG)* and has also served as a contributing writer for the *St. Louis Argus* newspaper.

ELIE GARDNER started at the Post-Dispatch as the online photo editor in July 2006. Now, she works as a night picture editor and staff photographer. After graduating from the Missouri School of Journalism, Gardner attended a six week journalism seminar at the Poynter Institute. Gardner enjoys working with pictures, whether she's shooting, editing or producing a project for the web. When she can't work with pictures, she enjoys walking her yellow lab Baley, reading, traveling, eating cupcakes and exploring the intricacies of the St. Louis community.

Acknowledgments

StudioSTL thanks Matt Picard for inviting our writers into his classroom. Ever-mindful of the fact that we entered a process that Matt initiated with these students in September, we are grateful for the opportunity to offer this writing collection as a reflection of the dedication and daily hard work of Matt and other teachers like him.

The Wellston writers seemed to know this book would happen well before StudioSTL and Mr. Picard discussed the possibility. They embraced the project and welcomed the StudioSTL mentoring team into their classroom from the first writing session until the final coffeehouse reading. They worked hard. We heard few grumbles and we saw few raised eyebrows. What we did hear were plenty of questions: "Is there too much repetition? Am I saying that word too much? Is our book good?" We saw twinkling eyes and smiles and downright pride when we read their words back to them. We are enormously proud of these seventh-graders who showed up on Thursday mornings to shine a bit of their light on the page.

Project Directors Tess Thompson and Jason Nicholas Vasser pooled their writing talents and mutual gifts for working with young people. Tess scheduled, coordinated, organized, and shared her poetry with her usual sparkle and an infectious enthusiasm for the project. We marveled at Jason's classroom gifts: teaching the kids Swahili, performing (not reading) his poetry, and sharing his thoughts in ways that made it safe for the students to express their own.

Only the finest kind of person will wake at the crack of dawn, drive across town in an ice storm, and – without exception – be a consistent presence for a young writer. Ah, our StudioSTL writing mentors! We are indebted to the Wellston team for coaching and coaxing in the classroom and for Saturday afternoon brainstorming sessions. We gratefully acknowledge:

BETTY BURNETT
RAE DRAIZEN
EMMA JEHLE
JEANNE SMITH
BRADEN WELBORN

StudioSTL writer/mentor Emma Jehle thanks the Saint Louis University Honors College and specifically, Lindsay Dencker, for making this great opportunity available. Rae Draizen wishes to thank Dr. Lauren Silver, professor at Washington University, who introduced her to StudioSTL. Project co-director Tess Thompson thanks Tom Rodebaugh for working hard for the team, and Ben Rodebaugh for sharing his mom with other kids on Thursday mornings.

Thanks to StudioSTL Anthology I authors Karissa Anderson and Devon Small who graciously read their published works and encouraged the Wellston writers, and to the other anthology authors whose self-portraits served as an inspiration for this book.

K. Curtis Lyle told us that he would be "honored" to pen a Foreword to the students' book of poetry, but it is truly StudioSTL that is honored to be able to include words from such a selfless poet and man of wisdom who, again and again, shares encouragement and time with young writers.

Julie Dill, a poet and our friend, provided copyediting and assembled the students' writing into a larger work. We are grateful for her usual excitement for our students' works and for her meticulous arrangement of their written pieces.

Elie Gardner, photographer, appeared at the back of the classroom one day and made herself invisible as her camera clicked. Elie's photographs capture the classroom, the students at work, and their dedication to their book. Elie has been a friend to StudioSTL in so many ways since the publication of Anthology I. We are endlessly grateful for her support and artistry.

We thank Mason Miller for offering his talent as a book designer and his ability to make each poem sing by itself, as art on a page, showcasing the students' work in a publication that they will treasure.

In early August 2005, a small group gathered around a coffee table and determined to start a writing center for ST. Louis youth and community. We are indebted to StudioSTL's founding Board of Directors for their dedication to the value of giving young writers a voice: Suzie Schmidt, Julia Feder, Erik Smetana, Pam Bliss, and Cherlyn Michaels.

The StudioSTL Board of Directors continues to build on the original Board's vision, which laid the foundation for this book and for a host of other student writing and publishing opportunities. Our heartfelt thanks to the ongoing support and hard work of the 2008 StudioSTL Board: Pam Bliss, Connie Farrow, Brooke Foster, John Pankey, Rachelle Rowe and Jeanne Smith.

We acknowledge the dedication of Rex Reed, Norm Moenkhaus and our friends at Youth Bridge Association for their partnership and support.

We are grateful to The Missouri Arts Council for their financial support of this publication, for permitting these students' voices to be heard, and for expanding awareness and appreciation of writing as Art. StudioSTL gratefully acknowledges the Regional Arts Commission for opening their doors as a sponsor for the book release events. We thank Lisette Dennis for her enthusiasm and for her support of young writers.

Finally, we thank Ms. Monica Stewart, Principal, Curtis Bishop Middle School and the Wellston teachers and staff who invited us into their school and always made us feel welcome and appreciated. We respect and admire their daily commitment to youth, to education, and to the Wellston community.

A note on the design of the book.

This book was designed by Mason Miller at the Punctilious Press studio in St. Louis. The text type is Joanna, titling type is Gill Sans, both designed by Eric Gill.